Contents

Look out for the paw-print icons. These tell you how long each project will take.

 = up to 30 minutes

 = up to 1 hour

 = more than 1 hour

Crazy about cats

If you're crazy about cats, you'll love the projects in this book. If you are lucky enough to have a pet cat, or just love those purr-fect faces, there is so much to make and do.

- ✪ Make gifts for friends or relatives
- ✪ Decorate your bedroom with cute cat designs
- ✪ Create homemade cat treats and playthings
- ✪ Throw a cat party!

At the back of the book you'll find a link to a web page packed with templates to use in the projects, and tips on how to use them to create designs of your own!

Getting started

Before starting each project, read the instructions carefully and make sure you have everything you need. Find out if you will need an adult to help with any of the steps. You must ask an adult first if you are planning to reuse or recycle an object, or decorate walls, clothes or furniture.

Mini mouse
page 20

Cake-pop cats
page 26

Shabby chic rug
page 14

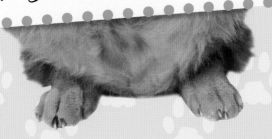

Cool CAT Projects

Loads of cool craft projects inside

Isabel Thomas

4721800023120 2

Raintree is an imprint of Capstone Global Library Limited, a company incorporated in England and Wales having its registered office at 7 Pilgrim Street, London, EC4V 6LB – Registered company number: 6695582

www.raintree.co.uk
myorders@raintree.co.uk

Edited by Helen Cox Cannons and Holly Beaumont
Designed by Philippa Jenkins
Picture research by Tracy Cummins
Production by Helen McCreath
Originated by Capstone Global Library Ltd
Printed and Bound in China by Leo Paper Group

ISBN 978 1 406 29820 8 (hardback)
19 18 17 16 15
10 9 8 7 6 5 4 3 2 1

ISBN 978 1 406 29825 3 (paperback)
20 19 18 17 16
10 9 8 7 6 5 4 3 2 1

British Library Cataloguing in Publication Data
A full catalogue record for this book is available from the British Library.

Acknowledgements
We would like to thank the following for permission to reproduce photographs:
iStockphoto: Linda Yolanda, Cover Bottom Left; Nova Development Corporation: Design Element; Shutterstock: Brooke Whatnall, Design Element, Lesha, 9 Bottom Right, Susan Schmitz, 1, Multiple Use, Vinogradov Illya, 7, Wallenrock, 29.

All other photography by Capstone Studio: Karon Dubke.

Every effort has been made to contact copyright holders of material reproduced in this book. Any omissions will be rectified in subsequent printings if notice is given to the publisher.

All the internet addresses (URLs) given in this book were valid at the time of going to press. However, due to the dynamic nature of the internet, some addresses may have changed, or sites may have changed or ceased to exist since publication. While the author and publisher regret any inconvenience this may cause readers, no responsibility for any such changes can be accepted by either the author or the publisher.

Safety instructions for adult helper
Some of the projects in this book involve steps that should only be carried out by an adult – these are indicated in the text. Always follow the instructions carefully.

ADULT HELP

Pet view

Look out for my tips on cat care as you work through the book!

Working safely

Work in an area where you can make a mess, using newspaper to protect the table or floor. Open the windows or go outside if you are using paint or glue. Keep pets away while you are crafting. Never use paint or glue near a pet – the fumes can be dangerous for animals.

Things... to keep in your craft kit

➤➤ Scissors, pens, pencils, paints, paintbrush, ruler, sticky tape and PVA glue.

➤➤ Pretty found objects such as feathers, stones and buttons.

➤➤ Scraps of pretty fabric, paper, card, newspapers and magazines.

➤➤ Boxes, jars and containers with interesting shapes (wash and dry food containers before storing them).

➤➤ Sewing materials such as needle and thread, wool, yarn, ribbons and trimmings.

Animal art projects

Cats have inspired artists since Egyptian times. Now it's your turn!

Drawing a purr-fect portrait

It can be hard to draw cats – they won't sit still unless they want to! Try this technique for drawing perfect pet portraits from photographs.

1 Using a permanent marker, draw a 15 × 15-cm (6 × 6-inch) grid of 1-cm squares on the plastic film. Clip it to a favourite cat photograph with paperclips.

2 Draw a matching grid on your drawing paper, in pencil. If you want to make your portrait larger than the photograph, double the length and width of each square.

3 Use the grid lines as a guide, transfer the main details from each square of the photograph to the corresponding square on the paper.

4 Remove the grid from the photograph and rub out the pencil gridlines, leaving the outline details. Use colouring pencils or pastels to complete the picture.

You will need:

- sheet of clear plastic film (try a stationery shop, or look out for clear plastic packaging)
- fine permanent marker pen
- cat photograph
- drawing paper and pencil
- ruler, rubber and paperclips

TOP TIP

It can be helpful to label the rows and columns with letters and numbers.

5 tips... for taking great cat photographs

Plan your cat photoshoot carefully, and show off your superstar pet.

➤➤➤ Take pictures in your cat's favourite locations. Your pet is more likely to be relaxed and in a good mood.

➤➤➤ If you are using a digital camera, turn off the sound and the flash. Your cat is less likely to get spooked and walk away.

➤➤➤ Get down so your camera is at cat's eye level. This might mean lying on the grass, or kneeling on the floor while your cat is up on a chair.

➤➤➤ Use a treat to encourage your cat to stay in one place. A sprinkle of catnip might encourage them to curl up on a favourite mat.

➤➤➤ Take pictures that show your pet's quirks. This will make your pictures unique, and help you capture your cat's personality.

You can't predict when your pet will strike the perfect pose, so keep a camera ready!

Elegant jewellery holder

Sharpen up your sculpting skills by making this cute salt-dough cat.

1 Mix the flour and salt together. Slowly add the water, stirring to make a dough. Knead (squeeze and mix) it with your hands for a few minutes.

2 Split the dough in half. Roll one half into a large ball-shaped body. Split the other half in half again, and roll one piece into a head, and the other into a fat, fluffy tail.

3 Assemble your cat by gently squashing and moulding the pieces together. If you want your cat's tail to be raised, push a cocktail stick inside the tail for support. Use the remaining dough to add ears and front paws. Roll three tiny balls to make a mouth and nose.

4 Leave the salt dough to dry out, or ask an adult to help you bake it in an oven at 165°C (329°F) for 1 hour.

You will need:

- 150 g (5 oz.) flour
- 75 g (2½ oz.) salt
- 60 ml water
- cocktail sticks
- paints and paintbrushes
- black marker pen
- diluted PVA glue (3 parts glue to 1 part water)

Pet view

Keep me away while you are crafting, especially if you are using paints or glue. Salt dough is safe for me to stand on if you would like to capture my paw print, but don't let me eat it!

5 Paint the cat in your favourite coat colours – tabby, tortoiseshell, grey or black, the choice is yours! When the paint has dried, use a marker pen to add tiny details.

6 Brush on a coat of watered-down PVA glue or clear varnish to seal your design.

TOP TIP

Use a cocktail stick to add tiny features, such as whiskers and eyes, while the dough is still wet. If you are not going to bake the salt dough, you could use beads for the eyes.

Use your cat as a handy holder for your favourite accessories.

Polymer clay pussycat

Salt dough is a great way to start sculpting, but for really detailed models you can use polymer clay. Try making cat key rings, bracelet charms and earrings.

Get crafty with paper

Let the world know you're crazy about cats with these purr-fect paper projects.

Cat's-eye card

Surprise cat lovers with this cheeky cat card. It's perfect for party invites, birthday cards, or a thank-you to the people who care for your cat when you're on holiday.

You will need:

- sheet of white paper
- pencil, ruler, scissors
- sheet of thin cardboard
- PVA glue
- colouring pens or pencils

1. Fold the paper in half along the long edge. Measure and mark a point ⅓ and ⅔ of the way along the fold. At each marked point, draw a 1 cm (½ in.) line from the fold, and carefully cut along it.

2. Mark the fold 1 cm (½ in.) on either side of the cut, and join the marks with the top of the cut to make a triangle. Fold the flaps back, along the lines, then repeat on the other side.

3. Open the paper and pinch either side of the diamond shapes so that they stick up. Now fold the paper again, to flatten the triangles inside.

4 Fold the cardboard in half along the long edge. Colour the area inside the fold black. Stick your folded paper into the folded card.

5 When the glue has dried, use colouring pens and pencils to complete your cat card.

Open the card and watch the cat wink!

HAPPY BIRTHDAY

Love from
Emily xxx

Pet view

Why not decorate a notebook and use it to keep a record of my health and habits? Knowing me really well will help you spot when I'm ill or injured.

Origami notelets

You can make these kitten cards in three simple folds. Choose paper the same colour as your cat, or cut a square of patterned or magazine paper.

1. Fold a square of paper in half from corner to corner, to make a downward facing triangle.

2. Make ears by folding up the left and right corners.

3. Fold down the top corner. Turn the paper over and draw eyes, nose and whiskers.

Remember to write a secret message inside!

Upcycle!

Recycling rubbish helps to protect the world for you and your cat, and it's great fun too. There are endless ways to turn waste packaging and craft materials into something cool for cats.

Make a cardboard cat den

Turn old cardboard boxes into a castle for your cat to explore. All you need is scissors, pens and a large imagination!

You will need:

- two or three large cardboard boxes (strong corrugated card is best)
- scissors
- black marker pen

You could add a floor with ramps for your cat to climb up.

Make sure the door is big enough for your cat to fit through.

Draw and cut out a doorway and windows on a large cardboard box.

Design a smaller cardboard den or tepee for your cat to sleep in.

5 ideas... for homemade cat toys

Cats and kittens love to play, and just like us they love new toys.

➤ Stuff an old sock with scrunched up newspaper and tie at the ankle. Add a pinch of dried catnip (page 19) for extra appeal.

➤ Hide dry cat treats or ping-pong balls inside cardboard boxes of different shapes and sizes, with small holes of different shapes and sizes. Your cat will have fun trying to find out what's inside.

➤ Turn a small rectangle of spare carpet into a scratching pad by punching a hole in the top, and hanging it from a wall hook, or looping it onto a chair or table leg using a ribbon or curtain ring.

➤ Take the handles off a paper bag to make a crunchy, scrunchy hiding place, or join several bags together to make a paper tunnel.

➤ Tie a scrap of felt to a bendy stick, and move it around for your cat to chase and pounce.

Fixing without tape or glue

Boxes can be joined together using the cardboard fixing template on the website (see page 31 for more information). Don't make the castle too high, in case it falls over when your cat is inside!

TOP TIP

If the card is very thick, ask an adult to help you with the cutting.

Pet view

I need exercise every day. Cat castles are great fun on a rainy day, and help indoor breeds stay fit and healthy without climbing the walls!

Shabby chic rug

This project is a great way to use up old T-shirts. Your cat will love curling up on a colourful rug that smells of home!

You will need:

- old T-shirts (you will need at least six – collect them from friends and family, or try charity shops)
- scissors
- chair or small table

1. Cut the hem off the bottom of a T-shirt. Now cut straight across the width of the T-shirt, 3 cm (1 in.) from the bottom, so that you have a loop of fabric. Repeat until you have around 12 loops (you may need two or more T-shirts).

2. Find a chair or table with legs slightly wider than your loops. Push each loop on to the legs, and space them out evenly to form your warp threads.

3. Now cut the rest of the T-shirts into strips around 3 cm (1 in.) wide. You can do this by cutting loops as above, then snipping through them to make long strips.

Warp threads

4. Stretch the strips holding one end in each hand and pulling. They will curl up into tubes.

5. Knot the first strip on to the bottom left warp thread, about 5 cm (2 in.) from the chair leg. Weave it loosely over and under the other warp threads, until you reach the top. Then go back the other way, weaving under the threads you went over on the way up.

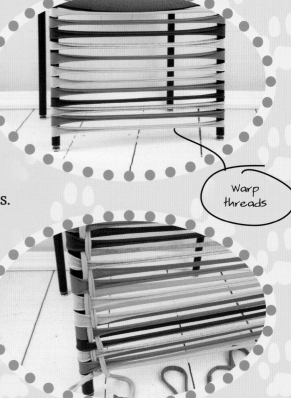

6 When you reach the end of a strip, simply knot another strip on, tucking the ends into the rug. Keep going until you are about 5 cm (2 in.) from the other chair leg, then knot the final strip to the last warp thread in the row.

7 Finish the rug by cutting and knotting each warp strip in turn.

You can knot two or more warp threads together in bunches.

T-shirt toy

If you don't have enough T-shirts to make a rug, try plaiting strips to make a cat toy instead.

TOP TIP

If you are using small T-shirts, knot several strips together to make longer strips.

Kitty kitchen

Every cat loves a treat, but did you know that some shop-bought and human treats are bad for cats? Try these delicious and healthy alternatives.

Plant a "cat garden"

Many cats love to nibble grass and other plants. Growing cat-friendly herbs inside can keep cats from nibbling houseplants that may harm them.

1 Fill a container two-thirds full with loose potting compost. Use a metal or ceramic container that your cat can't knock over.

2 Sprinkle your seeds over the surface of the compost, then cover with another thin layer. Water the seeds, then cover the container with a layer of cling film and keep it in a warm place. Remember to keep the compost damp.

3 Once seedlings have sprouted, move the container to a sunny spot, such as a windowsill, and keep it well watered.

4 When the plants are at least 8 cm (3 in.) tall (this takes about 10 days for wheatgrass), you can let your cat nibble straight from the pot.

You will need:
- seeds for one or more cat-friendly plants
- pretty container
- compost
- cling film

Pet view
Some cats spend their whole lives indoors. A container cat garden is a great way to give them access to fresh greens at any time of year.

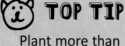 **TOP TIP**
Plant more than one cat garden, and rotate them so your cat always has fresh greens.

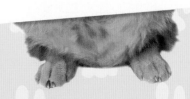

16

5 plants that cats love

Look out for these seeds in your nearest garden centre or pet shop.

- Catnip
- Oat grass
- Wheatgrass
- Barley grass
- Parsley

When you plant your seeds, make sure you follow the instructions on the packet.

Tasty tuna treats

Did you know that cows' milk can give cats an upset stomach? Make brilliant treats like these using rice milk instead.

1 Ask an adult to heat the oven to 175°C (350°F).

2 In a large bowl, mash the tuna with the flour.

3 In a separate bowl, mix the rice milk, oil and egg together with a fork.

4 Pour this mixture into the bowl with the flour and tuna, and use your hands to mix the ingredients into a sticky dough.

5 Break off small pieces of dough, roll each one into a ball shape, and place on a non-stick baking tray.

6 Ask an adult to help you bake the biscuits in the oven for 15 to 20 minutes.

7 Wait until the biscuits are completely cool, then store them in a tin or plastic box with a lid.

You will need:

- 1 small can of tuna in oil
- 100 g (3½ oz.) wholemeal flour
- 100 ml rice milk
- 1 tablespoon vegetable oil
- 1 egg

Sprinkle a little of your home grown catnip onto treats to make them irresistible!

5 projects... with homegrown catnip

Cats go crazy for the minty smell and taste of catnip! Here are five fun ways to treat your feline friends.

➤➤➤ Add chopped catnip to homemade treats.

➤➤➤ Dry a bunch of catnip by hanging it upside down in a dry, dark cupboard.

➤➤➤ Crumble up dried catnip and keep it in a plastic container. Place your cat's toys in the container overnight, or sprinkle a couple of pinches on a scratching post (page 24) or inside a den (page 12) to tempt your cat in.

➤➤➤ If you don't have a cat of your own, plant catnip in your garden to attract cat visitors!

➤➤➤ Use catnip to fill a stuffed cat toy (see page 20) as a treat for a cat, or as a scented cushion for your bedroom.

How to add your catnip

You can add the catnip in the recipe or sprinkle it on top of treats. Cats like it either way. Place in an airtight container and store in the fridge, or a cool, dry place.

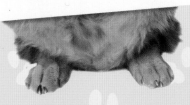

Pet view

I love sniffing and licking catnip, but watch out – it could make me feel full of energy, or super lazy. Once I'm over six months old, give me catnip just occasionally and stand back to let me enjoy it on my own.

Fantastic fabric projects

Collect scraps of fabric with pretty patterns and make this irresistible mouse.

Mini mouse

This little mouse is so cute, you won't be able to make just one!

1 Trace the mouse body template on the website (see page 31) and cut it out. Fold the fabric in half, printed side to printed side, and pin on the template with the straight edge along the fold. Cut around the template.

2 Keeping the mouse body folded, place the rope along the fold so that it just sticks out at the rounded end. Sew the edges together from tail to nose, to secure the rope. Stop when you are 2 cm (¾ in.) from the nose end.

3 Reach inside the nose and take hold of the rope. Pull to turn the mouse body inside out, so the printed side is showing.

You will need:
- 20 x 20 cm (8 x 8 in.) square of fabric
- needle and thread
- 15 cm (6 in.) of cord or rope
- stuffing
- catnip (optional)

 **TOP TIP**

You could also add eyes and whiskers using a marker pen!

4 Stuff the mouse body with the stuffing, sprinkling in some dried catnip as you go. Sew up the rest of the nose.

5 Trace the ear template and cut out two ears. You could use contrasting fabric. Sew on the ears, and add embroidery eyes, nose and whiskers.

If you haven't got a cat, make these mice as cute decorations or lavender bags!

Easy embroidery

Add cute cat designs to clothes, curtains or bags using this easy embroidery technique. Print and cut out one of the templates (see page 31), and use large stitches to tack the paper to the fabric. Thread a needle with embroidery thread, and stitch over the design with a tight running stitch. Snip the large tacking stitches and carefully cut or tear off the tracing paper to reveal your design.

Cat-tastic DIY projects

Even if your cat isn't allowed in your bedroom, fill it with reminders of your BFF (best feline friend!).

In a tail spin

You'll never forget feeding time with this cat-tastic clock.

1. Measure the distance between the centre of the clock and the top. Cut out a cardboard cat silhouette of this height. You could scale up a template (see page 31), or create your own. Decorate the shape to match the coat of your favourite cat.

2. Cut out a matching tail shape, scaling it up so it's the same length as the minute hand of your clock mechanism.

3. Take the battery out of the clock, so that the hands stop moving while you work on the project. Stick the cat shape to the clock face.

4. Using strong glue, stick the tail shape along the length of the minute hand.

5. When the glue has dried, replace the battery in the clock, and reset the time.

You will need:

- old wall clock
- strong glue
- scissors
- cardboard

After all that work, it might be time for a catnap!

Making shapes

Stencilling is an easy way to give walls and furniture a chic cat makeover. Print one of the templates and transfer it to a piece of thick card. Carefully cut out the shape, leaving a cat-shaped hole. You can use scissors for this or ask an adult to do it for you using a craft knife.

1 Attach the stencil to the surface you want to decorate using masking tape, then sponge paint over the hole.

2 When the paint has dried, gently remove the stencil by peeling off the tape.

You can use your stencil over and over again to create cool cat patterns.

TOP TIP

Always check with an adult before painting walls or furniture.

Claw-some fun

Make a scratching post from scratch!

1 Use the template from the website (see page 31) to cut out 100 identical shapes from thick card. Cut a hole in the middle of each one.

2 Ask an adult to help you attach your wooden dowel to the base, by screwing through the bottom of the base and into the dowel.

3 Simply slot your cardboard shapes on to the dowel, and your scratching post is ready to play with.

You will need:

- lots of corrugated cardboard (collect some old boxes)
- scissors
- 50 cm (20 in.) of wooden dowel
- piece of wood for a base (e.g. an old drawer front)

😺 TOP TIP

Ask an adult to help you use a tool called a *hole saw* to cut the holes more quickly. The holes should be the same diameter as your dowel.

When the scratching post wears out, simply slot on fresh squares of card!

Puzzle feeder

Make mealtimes more interesting with these homemade puzzle feeders.

Cut holes of different sizes in a cardboard tube or box, place some dried cat food inside, and fold up the ends. Can your cat work out how to get it out by rolling the tube around?

Goodbye to boring bowls!

Make a larger puzzle feeder using short and tall cardboard tubes in different combinations. Watch your cat as they feed, to make sure they are nibbling the food and not the tubes!

Pet view

In the wild, cats have to hunt for their food. A puzzle feeder helps me exercise my brain and body every day.

Throw a cat party!

Your cat is part of the family, so make him or her part of holidays and celebrations, too.

Cake-pop cats!

These bite-sized cakes are super-cute and super-yummy.

1. Crumble the cake into a mixing bowl to make fine crumbs. Mix two tablespoons of icing with the crumbs. Add more buttercream icing, one spoonful at a time, until the mixture sticks together like dough.

2. Break off small pieces of the dough and roll them into balls. Put the balls into a fridge for an hour. Ask an adult to help you melt the white and milk chocolate while you're waiting.

3. When the balls of cake are firm, take them out of the fridge. Dip the end of each stick into the melted chocolate, and push it into a ball of cake.

4. Holding the stick, dip the ball of cake into the melted chocolate. Roll it gently from side to side until it is completely covered.

You will need:
- sponge cake
- buttercream icing
- melted white and milk chocolate
- wooden or rolled paper sticks
- chocolate buttons
- pink heart-shaped sprinkles, sweets and writing icing to decorate
- colander

 TOP TIP

Before dipping, use your fingers to pinch ear shapes at the top of each ball.

5 Carefully slot the stick into the colander to hold it in place. It doesn't matter if some chocolate trickles down – this will help to keep the cake-pop on the stick.

6 Repeat steps 3 to 5 until you have coated every cake ball. Put the cake-pops in the fridge to set.

7 When the first layer of chocolate has set, add markings by dipping each ear or nose in a different shade of melted chocolate.

8 When the cake-pops have set, use sprinkles, sweets or writing icing to add noses, eyes and whiskers. Pop the cake-pops back in the fridge until you are ready to serve them.

Use different combinations of milk and white chocolate to make different coloured cats!

Crafty party favours

These DIY cake-pop jars make a great going-home gift for your party guests.

1 Measure out the dry ingredients for making cake-pop cats.

2 Carefully add them to each jar in neat layers.

3 Put the chocolate buttons and decorations in sealed food bags so they don't get mixed up.

4 Finally, tie on a label with instructions for making the cake-pops at home!

You will need:

- clean, empty jars
- dry ingredients for cake-pop cats (see page 26)
- edible decorations
- sealed food bags
- labels and ribbon

Use playful decoration colours for a rainbow cat parade!

Meow

Pet view

If you want me to be at the party, please keep the guest list small. I get nervous around large groups of people I don't know. If you'd like to throw a cat-crazy birthday party for all your friends, why not tell me about it afterwards?

5 gift ideas... for cat lovers

These projects make great gifts for cat owners, and double up as party favours!

⇢ Make the origami notelets on page 11, and use them as party invitations or place names.

⇢ The fabric mice on pages 20–21 can be embroidered with the cat or owner's initials.

⇢ Decorate small paper bags with cat faces and paper ears, and fill them with dry cat treats.

⇢ The winking cat cards on page 10 make purr-fect thank you cards!

⇢ Cover cheap picture frames or pencil pots with cat pictures and varnish with PVA glue for a gift so stylish, no one will guess how simple it was to make!

Cat facts

5 facts... for cat lovers

- A fifth of UK households have a pet cat – that's around 8.5 million cats!
- Some white cats have one orange eye and one blue eye. They are usually deaf in the ear next to the blue eye.
- Devon Rexes are the only cats that wag their tails when they are happy. Other cats wag their tails when they are angry or scared.
- The ancient Egyptians were the first people to keep pet cats.
- A cat can double its paw size by extending its claws!

Find out more

The Cats Protection League has a website full of games and activities for cat fans!
www.cats.org.uk/cats-for-kids

Visit the RSPCA for tips on caring for your feline friends.
www.rspca.org.uk/adviceandwelfare/pets/cats

Find out all about cats' beautiful coats and colours at the International Cat Association.
www.tica.org

Battersea Cats & Dogs Home has a website with educational resources and lots of things to make and do.
www.battersea.org.uk

Templates

Visit **www.raintree.co.uk/content/download** and select "Cool Cat Projects" to download free templates to use with the projects in this book. You can also use them to create your own cat designs. Once you have printed a template, follow these tips to transfer it to the material you are working with.

- Use masking tape to hold a sheet of tracing or baking paper over your chosen design and draw over the outline with a soft pencil.

- Tape the paper on to the surface you'd like to transfer the picture to.

- Draw over the lines using a pen with a hard point.

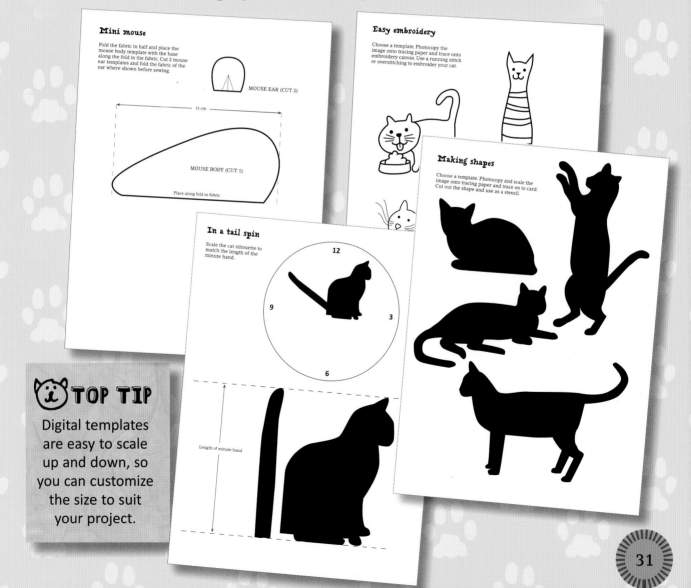

Mini mouse

Fold the fabric in half and place the mouse body template with the base along the fold in the fabric. Cut 2 mouse ear templates and fold the fabric of the ear where shown before sewing.

MOUSE EAR (CUT 2)

15 cm

MOUSE BODY (CUT 1)

Place along fold in fabric

Easy embroidery

Choose a template. Photocopy the image onto tracing paper and trace onto embroidery canvas. Use a running stitch or overstitching to embroider your cat.

Making shapes

Choose a template. Photocopy and scale the image onto tracing paper and trace on to card. Cut out the shape and use as a stencil.

In a tail spin

Scale the cat silhouette to match the length of the minute hand.

12

9

3

6

Length of minute hand

TOP TIP

Digital templates are easy to scale up and down, so you can customize the size to suit your project.

Index